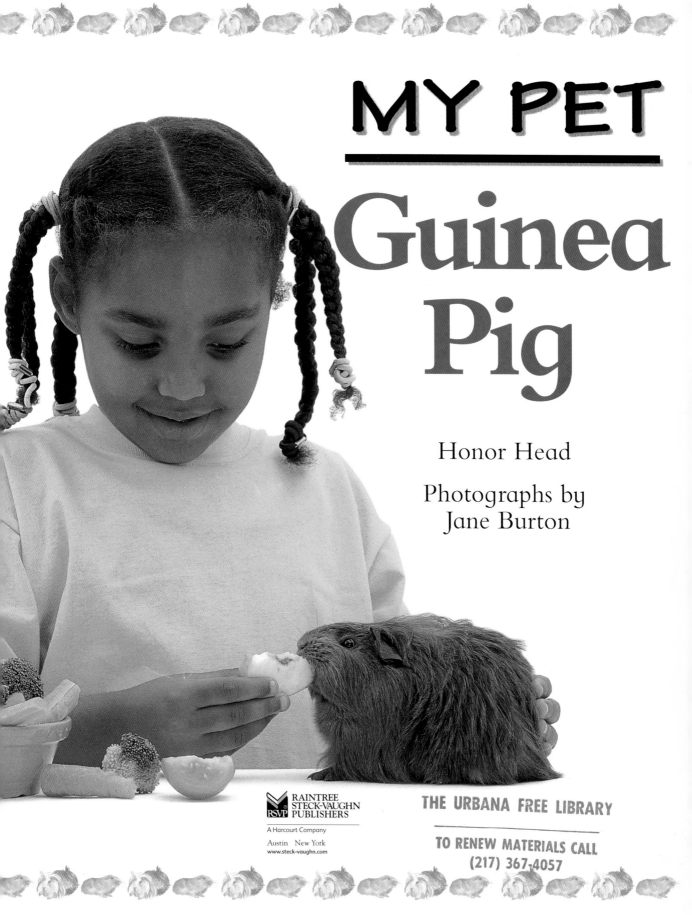

MY PET

Guinea Pig

Honor Head

Photographs by
Jane Burton

RAINTREE
STECK-VAUGHN
PUBLISHERS

A Harcourt Company

Austin   New York
www.steck-vaughn.com

Published by Raintree Steck-Vaughn
Publishers, an imprint of Steck-Vaughn
Company.

Editors: Claire Edwards, Erik Greb
Art Director: Max Brinkmann
Designer: Rosamund Saunders
Illustrator: Pauline Bayne

Printed in Singapore

1 2 3 4 5 6 7 8 9 0 LB 03 02 01 00

**Library of Congress Cataloging-in-Publication
Data**

Head, Honor.
  Guinea pig/Honor Head; photographs by Jane
Burton.
   p. cm.—(My pet)
  Summary: Describes the physical
characteristics and habits of guinea pigs and tells
how to care for them as pets.
  ISBN 0-7398-2888-6 (hardcover)
  ISBN 0-7398-3009-0 (softcover)
  1. Guinea pigs—Juvenile literature. [1. Guinea pigs.
2. Animals—Infancy. 3. Pets.] I. Burton, Jane, ill.
II. Title.

SF459.G9 H396 2000
                          00–027050

Contents

Owning Your Own Pet 5

Different Types of Guinea Pigs 6

A Pregnant Guinea Pig 8

Newborn Guinea Pigs 10

Hutches and Runs 12

Settling In 14

Handling Your Guinea Pig 16

Feeding Your Guinea Pig 18

Cleaning the Hutch 20

Taking Care of Your Guinea Pig 22

Visiting the Vet 24

A Friend for Your Guinea Pig 26

Growing Old 28

Words to Remember 30

Index 31

Notes for Parents 32

My Guinea Pig

ear

whiskers

coat

claws

It's fun to have your own pet.

Guinea pigs make good pets and are fun to play with. But they need to be looked after carefully.

Guinea pigs need to be fed every day, and their hutch needs to be kept clean. You must be gentle with guinea pigs because they can be easily frightened. Your pet may be with you for a long time.

Young children with pets should always work with an adult. For further notes, please see page 32.

There are many different types of guinea pigs.

Some guinea pigs have short, smooth hair. Others have ruffled or long hair.

Long-haired guinea pigs are harder to care for. They need lots of grooming.

Guinea pigs need company and like to play together.

Some guinea pigs are just one color. Others have patches and stripes.

A guinea pig's hair is called a coat.

A pregnant guinea pig needs peace and quiet.

When a guinea pig is pregnant, she will eat more. She will also need more water to drink.

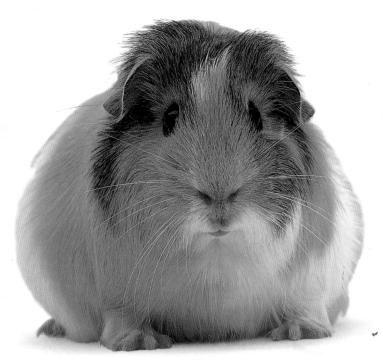

Just before she has her babies, the mother guinea pig needs to be left alone and handled very carefully.

A guinea pig has about
three babies. She licks
them clean as soon
as they are born.

**A pregnant guinea pig will
need a little bread
soaked in milk,
along with her
normal food.**

Baby guinea pigs are born with all their fur.

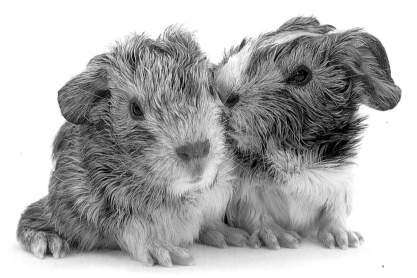

A newborn guinea pig looks like its mother. Its eyes are open, and it has all its teeth.

Newborn guinea pigs drink their mother's milk right away. This is called suckling.

Baby guinea pigs suckle until they are about three weeks old. They also begin to eat solid food after one or two days.

When guinea pigs are one week old, they can move around very quickly.

This baby guinea pig is three weeks old. He will be old enough to leave his mother at five weeks.

Your guinea pig will need a warm hutch to live in.

A hutch should have one part you can see into and one part that is closed off, where your guinea pig can sleep.

If the hutch is outside, make sure it is sheltered from rain and wind. It should be waterproof and raised off the ground. Bring it inside in cold weather.

Put a layer of newspaper on the bottom of the hutch. Add wood shavings on the top. Put plenty of hay in the sleeping area.

Your guinea pig should have a run where it can scurry around. Make sure the run is strong, so that it cannot be knocked over.

Your guinea pig will need time to settle in.

When you show your guinea pig its new home, it may feel scared. Leave it alone for a little while until it is used to you.

Your guinea pig will enjoy exploring. Give it some toys to play with.

Cut some holes in a box for your pet to crawl through. Hide some food for it in a large flowerpot.

Your guinea pig needs to be cared for every day. If you are going on vacation, ask a friend to take care of your pet. Give your friend everything your guinea pig will need. Carry your guinea pig in a special carrier.

Your guinea pig will enjoy being picked up.

Always be gentle and quiet with your guinea pig. Loud noises and sudden movements will frighten it. Talk to it quietly, so that it grows used to your voice.

If your guinea pig is happy, it may chirp or purr.

When you pick up your guinea pig, stroke it gently. Kneel down. Put one hand around the guinea pig's chest and the other hand under its bottom to lift it.

Do not squeeze your guinea pig. If it struggles, put it down immediately. Never drop your guinea pig – you will hurt it. Always put it down on the ground.

Give your guinea pig lots of nice things to eat.

Feed your guinea pig some fresh fruit and vegetables every day. Give it plenty of mixed greens but not lettuce. Always wash fresh food carefully.

Give your pet special guinea pig food twice a day.

Fruits and vegetables will help to keep your guinea pig healthy. You can also pick wild plants for your pet, but you need to check which kinds are safe.

Buy your guinea pig a water bottle and keep it filled with fresh water all the time. Make sure the spout is metal, because guinea pigs chew their bottles.

Keep your guinea pig's hutch clean.

Clean your guinea pig's hutch once a day. Take out dirty bedding and old food. Make sure the hay is clean and that there is enough to make a cozy bed.

Clean your pet's water bottle at least once a week with a bottle brush. Wash the food bowl every day.

Scrub out the hutch once a week
with germ killer from a pet store.
Put in clean paper, wood shavings,
and bedding. Wear rubber gloves,
or wash your hands afterward.

**Scrub out the hutch more
often when the weather
is hot. Dry it carefully
before you put the
new bedding in.**

Have fun taking care of your guinea pig.

Brush your guinea pig's coat gently in the direction the fur grows. Use a soft brush. If your guinea pig has long or rough fur, brush it every day with a stiff brush. This is called grooming.

Guinea pigs with short hair lick themselves clean, but they still like to be groomed.

You can buy a mineral block for your guinea pig. Minerals help to keep your guinea pig healthy.

A well-fed, healthy guinea pig has silky, clean-smelling fur, bright eyes and clean ears and nose.

Your guinea pig may need to visit the vet.

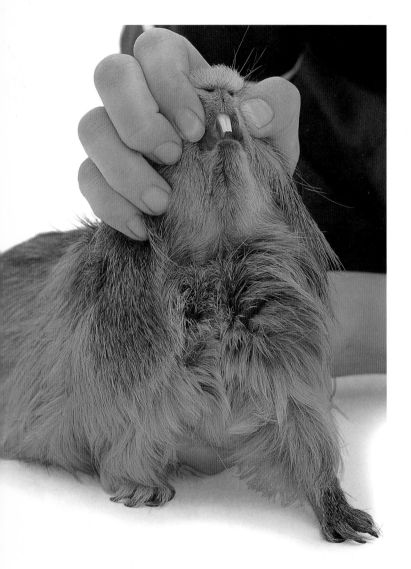

Your vet will be able to answer any questions you have about your guinea pig's health. If your pet is sick, the vet may give it some medicine. The vet may also check your pet's teeth to make sure they are not too long.

Give your guinea pig a block of wood to gnaw on. This will help to keep its front teeth sharp and not too long.

If your guinea pig's claws grow too long, your vet will clip them for you.

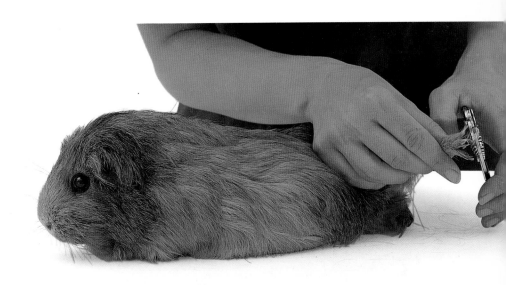

Check your pet's fur to make sure that there are no little insects in it. If there are, buy some powder from the vet. When you use the powder, cover your pet's face with one hand.

Your guinea pig will need a friend.

Guinea pigs do not like living
alone. The best friend for your
guinea pig is another guinea pig.
Two females or two males from
the same litter will get along well.

Rabbits get along well with guinea pigs if they are introduced when they are both young.

Your guinea pig will enjoy meeting your friends. Make sure you are not too noisy when you are with your guinea pig. Do not run around with it.

Your guinea pig may live for up to seven years.

As your guinea pig grows old, make especially sure it is kept warm. Check your guinea pig every day, especially its ears, eyes, and nose. Call your vet if you are worried about anything.

As your guinea pig grows older, it will sleep more and play less.

Guinea pigs usually live for about five years. Like people, they grow old and die. You may feel sad when this happens, but you will be able to look back and remember all the happy times you had with your guinea pig.

Words to Remember

bedding Material for your pet to sleep in.

coat The name for a guinea pig's fur.

groom To brush an animal's fur to keep it clean.

hutch A wooden house where pets such as guinea pigs live.

mineral block A special type of food for your guinea pig.

run A type of large hutch where guinea pigs can run around.

suckling When a baby guinea pig drinks its mother's milk, it is suckling.

vet A doctor for animals.

Newborn guinea pigs are like tiny adults.

Newborn.

One week old.

Three weeks old.

Index

baby guinea pigs 10–11

birth 8–9

claws 25

cleaning 20–21

food 5, 8, 9, 18–19

grooming 22

holding a guinea pig 17

health 23, 24–25

hutches 12, 13

suckling 10

teeth 24

vets 24–25

water 8, 19, 20

Notes for Parents

Guinea pigs make excellent pets and will give you and your family a great deal of pleasure. But keeping any animal is a big responsibility. If you decide to buy guinea pigs for your child, you will need to ensure that they are healthy, happy, and safe. You will also have to care for your pets if they are sick, and help your child with them until he or she is at least five years old. It is your responsibility to make sure your child does not harm the guinea pigs and learns to handle them correctly.

Here are some other points to think about before you decide to own a guinea pig:

* Do you have somewhere to keep your guinea pigs away from drafts and direct sunshine?
* Guinea pigs can live for up to seven years. You may have to pay vet's bills if they are sick.
* If you go on vacation, you will need to make sure someone can care for the guinea pigs while you are away.

* Do you have other pets? Will the guinea pigs get along with them? Cats and dogs will usually frighten guinea pigs. Keep them apart.
* You should never keep a guinea pig by itself. Males from the same litter can be kept together, as can females from the same litter. Don't keep males and females together because this will result in unwanted litters.
* Guinea pigs fed on the latest complete diets should not be fed mineral supplements unless the vet tells you to do so.

This book is only an introduction for young readers. If you have any questions about how to care for your pet guinea pig, you can contact the Humane Society of the U.S., 2100 L Street NW, Washington, DC 20037.